READ ANY GOOD BOOKS?

Sinclair B. Ferguson

D1796096

THE BANNER OF TRUTH TRUST

THE BANNER OF TRUTH TRUST
3 Murrayfield Road, Edinburgh EH12 6EL
P.O Box 621, Carlisle, Pennsylvania 17013, USA

*

© The Banner of Truth Trust 1992
First Published 1992
ISBN 0 85151 633 5

*

Typeset in 10½/12 Linotron Plantin
at The Spartan Press Ltd,
Lymington, Hants
Printed in Great Britain by
Howie and Seath Ltd, Edinburgh

The final words of Paul's written ministry are both poignant and illuminating. They are deeply poignant in their appeal to Timothy to visit him in his Roman prison: poignant too, in the apostle's request that his younger friend should come before winter and bring the cloak Paul had left at Troas. Illuminating are the other items the apostle wanted to have beside him – 'my scrolls, especially the parchments' (2 *Tim*.4:13). Facing certain death, he still believed there was value in reading.

THE POWER OF THE PRINTED WORD

Throughout history people have recognized the power of ideas. From the beginning of the Christian church the apostles recognized the power of ideas written and disseminated in the form of literature.

In our strongly visual age we have become less conscious of that. But pick up an old edition of a Christian book which tells you the number of copies of it in print. The figures will probably astonish you. For our Christian forefathers realized that the printing press was a powerful instrument for teaching and spreading the Christian gospel.

In the past, the people of God made widespread use of the printed word. Yet few Western Christians think there is any spiritual importance in the question: 'Read any good books?'

It would be wrong to exaggerate the significance of the

question. Some of us, by nature and upbringing, are avid readers. We would have been even if we had never become Christians. Others find little pleasure in any kind of book. Yet the question does indicate how seriously we take the biblical challenge to grow in knowledge and understanding. It reveals how important we think it is to develop a biblically instructed mind.

BOOKS AND THE HEALTH OF THE CHURCH

If we complain to our doctor of a general lethargy, he may well ask us about our diet and our appetite: Are we getting enough protein? Do we eat enough fruit? Is there enough roughage in the diet? Is it balanced? To some extent our 'intake' and our 'output' are closely related. The same is true of 'intake' and 'output' in the Christian life.

Christian history, biography and personal experience show us that Christians who read have tended to be stronger Christians than they otherwise would have been. The use of books has been one of the marks of the spiritual vitality and health of the Christian church. In fact, what we discover in many biographies is that those who have been the greatest Christian activists have also been the most prolific producers of and readers of Christian literature.

Early in his ministry, Martin Luther, the reformer, had little time for Christian literature. Like others since, he tended to regard Christian literature as antagonistic to the spirit of the gospel. The gospel, he said, is about the preached word and we must preach. Yet that same Martin Luther (incredible though it seems) was responsible for one-third of all the books published in the German language in the first half of the sixteenth century! On every bookshelf in Germany, one out of every three books was probably authored by Luther!

Why was this? Luther saw that by writing he could spread the message of the gospel and the joy of the Reformation; by reading Christian people would grow in grace and the church of Jesus Christ would be built up and strengthened.

Think about biographies you have read. Isn't it true that the majority of greatly-used Christians were men and women who were always using, in one sense or another, printed material? Thus, in the purposes of God, using Christian literature has been a sign of vitality in the people of God.

There are many reasons for this. One is that the Christian faith is a faith of the mind. Faith is not a mindless activity; it involves understanding the gospel. Not that it requires a high IQ in order to be a Christian, but the *renewing* of the mind (*Rom.*12:1-2) is essential for the transformation of your life.

YOU ARE WHAT YOU READ!

We often hear the slogan, 'You are what you eat'. Most Christians become what they read. This is true primarily as we study God's Word. But it is also true of reading books which will shed light on God's Word; books which will search our consciences from God's Word, and will challenge us to a new obedience to it.

The Christian faith involves knowing God. In its very nature it is a faith that is related to reading, understanding and obeying God's Word. It is inevitable that active Christians have often been prolific readers, and frequently prolific writers.

Think of John Knox as an example. He was, surely, one of the great activists of the Christian church, and yet he saw the tremendous significance of putting his ideas into print in order that they might be spread.

Think of Richard Baxter of Kidderminster, who wrote more books than many Christians would have sufficient shelf space to contain – and all because he recognized how much God is able to do through the literature that his people write and disseminate.

Think of John Owen, or George Whitefield; think of John Wesley and his vision of producing a basic library of great Christian classics for all Christians to read; think of Robert Murray M'Cheyne or the Bonar brothers. Think too of older Christians to whom you owe a great deal – we have illustrations everywhere we look, of men who have been conscious of the need to spread the Word of God by means of the printed page.

From one point of view, there has never been a generation which has possessed such an abundance of Christian literature. The question today is not: Where are we to find good books? Rather, it is: How best can we use these Christian books? It can be answered in several ways.

1: Why use Christian Books?

The most obvious reason is that there is value in reading. Perhaps you know the famous words from Francis Bacon's essay 'Of Studies': 'Reading maketh a full man', he wrote. He meant that about reading in general. Reading promotes maturity in our lives; it fills our minds with new thoughts; it enables us to be more fully and truly human, better equipped for this world than we otherwise would be.

If that is the effect of reading in general, how much more important it is that Christians should read books which help to bring us to the measure of the stature of the fullness of Christ (*Eph*.4:13). What books can be more important than those which have as their goal the glory of God, and the transformation of our lives into the image of Jesus Christ, and the reaching of men and women with the gospel to the praise of God's glorious grace?

Books can help us enormously in our Christian lives. This is true in different ways and for different reasons.

(1) READING TO RECEIVE

By reading we expose ourselves to the ministry that Jesus Christ has given to the whole church. Paul's principle (expounded in Ephesians chapter 4) is that the ascended Christ gives a variety of gifts to the church. He thus displays his own glory in his people, in both their character and lifestyle.

All the gifts Christ has given to the church are necessary if we are to reflect the full glory of our incomparable Saviour. When Paul expounds that principle in Ephesians 4, he stresses that Christ has given to the church the permanent ministry of pastors and teachers.

We are accustomed to associating those ministries with the ministry of the local congregation. But Paul has a larger vision than that. He is speaking about God's gift in Christ to the whole church: all pastors, all teachers, are gifts of the ascended Christ to the whole church.

When teaching and exhorting gifts are exercised in writing, they can edify and encourage us even although we may be separated by great distance or by time from (or, in the case of translations, even by language) the author.

Think of that when you next take a book into your hands! You can sit under the ministry of Augustine, or Calvin, or John Owen, or Baxter, or Bunyan, or Edwards, or Boston, or Spurgeon! Even those who are dead may yet speak to you and by their exposition of God's truth help forge you into the kind of man or woman that was produced in earlier days by their living testimony and ministry.

Paul prays in Ephesians 3:18 that Christians will come to understand the height and the depth, the breadth, and length of the love of Christ *together with all the saints*. We need all the saints and all the insights that Christ has given to them in his word if we are to appreciate the full riches of his grace. In his providence God has made that possible by the ministry of Christian literature.

In our own time, in a way that exceeds all expectations, you can benefit from the richest gifts that Jesus Christ has given to the church, by going into a bookshop, and handing over a few pieces of paper or metal coins!

Compare your privileges with those of the early Christians. In the first century, the cost of the 'paper' alone for one copy of the New Testament amounted to an entire year's wages. Christian literature was simply not available to the average Christian. Today, in the West, for a fraction of the average daily wage, you can buy a Christian book. What a privilege it is to live in such an environment, where you can receive the ministry that Christ has given to the whole church! Does that not make you want to make use of the privileges you have?

(2) BOOKS FOR GIVING

By means of Christian literature you can introduce others to the gospel. Books can go where you cannot go, and (sometimes just as important!) books can stay where you have already outstayed your welcome. If you leave a book with someone, it will remain with them when you have left.

You cannot sit for ever beside the brokenhearted or confused, but the book may be there for them to stretch out their hands and use. You cannot go on for ever pursuing in person those who have backslidden, but a book may pursue them with the help of your prayers. Neither you nor the pastoral leaders in your congregation have all the time they need to explain the gospel or the teaching of Scripture, or the application of the message to every individual. But every individual may have at his hand a book that will help them. Most people who have used Christian literature in this way have seen God use books in the lives of others.

I vividly remember a period when Professor John Murray's book, *Redemption – Accomplished and Applied* was out of print. A student told me that it had been recom-

6

mended to him, but his search for a copy had proved fruitless. I happened to possess two jealously-guarded copies, and sent one to him. Some months later it was returned. He had read the book several times. The whole direction of his thinking had been transformed.

I have personally been very slow to leave books with bereaved people. But this week I visited a mourning family. They quoted parts of a book a Christian friend had left with them. It had clearly helped them enormously. I learned an important lesson.

These are but illustrations of a principle: we may use Christian literature where we ourselves cannot go; we may say through good books what others have said much better than we ourselves ever could.

(3) BOOKS ABROAD

We need to catch a vision of the value and power of the printed word – not only for our own personal use, but for its international use, and for the way in which we pray for Christian literature.

Many fine books are translated into other languages where there are relatively few Christian books. These books can go where neither you nor the author will ever go. In various parts of the world today there are diligent Christian people translating literature into their own language. Books are being sold and given away to people who are hungry to read something, and have almost nothing to read. We need to promote this ministry, not only personally, but also in prayer and by our giving.

So we should use Christian literature, both for what it does to ourselves by God's grace and what it may accomplish by that same grace in the world in which we live.

This brings us to a second important question.

2: What kind of Christian Books should we use?

It would, of course, be quite wrong for a church or individual to require that every Christian should read a prescribed list of books. But it is important to have some fixed principles in our thinking.

If you are a mother, you probably have (or feel you ought to have!), some fixed principles about the way in which you are going to feed yourself and your household – however informally they are worked out. In most families, you need to be a good steward of both what is available in the supermarket and what is possible within your family budget! The same is true of our diet of Christian reading. We need certain simple but clear fixed principles that will help us to profit from our Christian reading. Here are four suggested guidelines.

(1) READ THE GREAT BOOKS

That is worth repeating: Read the great books!

In his preface to an English translation of Athanasius' great work *On the Incarnation*, C.S. Lewis comments on our mistaken modesty. When we want, for example, to find out something about Plato, we tend to go to the local library or bookshop and ask for 'a book about Plato'. But, wrote Lewis, that is the greatest mistake we can possibly make, for this reason: we will almost certainly find the book *about* Plato far more difficult to understand than reading Plato himself! You may have discovered this yourself. Books *about* books are often neither as helpful nor as clear as the original, 'the real thing'.

Read 'the real thing'! Saying this is not to despise abridgements, simplifications and popularizations, the 'Little Pilgrim's Progress', 'Select writings of . . .' or 'An anthology of. . ..'

It is worth emphasizing that the greatest books in the Christian church are usually very readable. You should bear in mind why they were written: great books were written to show a great God and a great Christ to the people of God. You must never let yourself be tricked into reading lesser books about great subjects when you are perfectly capable of reading great books about great subjects! As you will discover, they are very often among the clearest and most enjoyable to read.

So, read the great books. Read the great books on Jesus Christ. Read the great books about God; read the great books on sin. Remember that in most cases they were written for people just like ourselves.

As you read, remember to have a proper, balanced diet. You need solid meat that you can get your teeth into – books that will stretch your mind and strengthen your understanding and love of God.

Have you ever read the *Institutes of the Christian Religion*, by John Calvin? Now, there is a work whose reputation and length sometimes frightens us off from even beginning it. But pick it up (especially in the visually more pleasant translation by Ford Lewis Battles) and you will find it far easier to read than you feared. It is far more heart-warming, far more instructive, far more Christian than you ever imagined! And worth a box full of recent paperbacks!

(2) READING ACCORDING TO A PLAN

Christian reading is like Christian giving. As you give to the work of God's kingdom on Sunday morning, you may feel your gifts are small and feeble. But when you give according to plan, you begin to realize, 'In God's providence I have this year in which to give, and I have this proportion of my total income to give to the Lord's work'. It can be quite a surprise to see just how much there is for you to give.

The same is true of Christian literature. Unless we read according to plan, we may feel, 'Well, I have so little time to read, there is no point in reading these great books; I will stick to the small, easily-read ones.'

When you make a plan and you read regularly – an hour each day, or time spent on the bus or train, or a section at lunchtime, you will be amazed how much you are able to get through, and how much you learn. You will begin to realize, as you look back on a year, 'Why, I have read the whole of the *Institutes*; I have read a short work by the great John Owen; I have been challenged by the *Life of Henry Martyn*'. And as you read according to plan you will begin to discover that your reading is beginning to make you a 'full man', a more spiritually mature woman.

(3) READ SELECTIVELY

Francis Bacon in that famous essay 'Of Studies' also comments: 'Some books are to be tasted, others to be swallowed whole, and some few to be chewed and digested.' That is true of Christian literature as well. Being a good reader does not mean having read many books, but knowing some good books, and having mastered your best and greatest books.

We need to read selectively for a variety of reasons.

One of them is this: it is all too easy to become lovers of books – possessing them and reading them – yet not to grow as lovers of God. Large libraries, knowledge of the latest thing – these can co-exist with a lack of growth and depth in character development and grace. Book-lovers can become like butterflies, flitting from one flower to the next.

As Christians we ought not to be so naïve as to think that publishers are unaware of the habits of Christian purchasers to buy what they may not read, or to buy a book simply because it is recent! Perhaps before you became a Christian it was the latest golf club you needed to have, or the latest car. Do not assume that your desire to possess the latest Christian book is necessarily a spiritual characteristic!

Read selectively, then, in the sense of reading in order to digest, understand and put into practice what you learn from Scripture through the books you read. Master a few; treasure them; study them; know them. For it is only as you know them that you will be able to use them further for God's glory.

(4) READ A BALANCED VARIETY OF BOOKS

Vary your reading. A balanced diet is a very obvious dietetic principle. We do not eat the same thing every day! It is not just that your meals would become unattractive; in addition you could develop some kind of vitamin deficiency, or other problem.

Biblical and theological reading

We need to apply the same principle to our reading. We must, for example, balance our biblical reading as well as our theological reading; our use of books on the text of Scripture with our use of books on the doctrine and theology of Scripture.

Why is that important? It is vital for us as Christians to have an accurate understanding of the doctrines of the gospel. But it is important that the spirit in which we hold that teaching should also be born out of and nourished by our understanding of Scripture.

Do you understand that principle? Those of us who admire and value the great systematic theologies must always remember that they must never be loved with the affection we have for Scripture itself. They are not Scripture, nor do they have the same spirit as the Spirit who inspired the sacred text of Scripture. We need to drink deeply of that Spirit, as we seek to breathe in the instruction of godly men and women.

It is significant that Paul says to Timothy that he is to guard the good deposit 'in faith *and love*' (2 *Tim.*1:13). It is not just a matter of guarding the good deposit intellectually. We must guard it in a spirit that illustrates the quality and the fruitfulness of that good deposit in faith and love.

If we are to be moulded intellectually, spiritually and emotionally by the spirit as well as the propositional teaching of Scripture, it is important for us in our reading to read commentaries and studies that shed light directly on the text of Scripture or, more accurately, are able to help us to see the light that springs forth from the text of Scripture.

When, in the mid-seventeenth century the Westminster Divines wrote about the necessary characteristics of preaching, they emphasized that the listeners should be able to see how the teaching in the sermon came specifically from the text which was being expounded. We need to be able to do that too, so that our faith may be grounded in the Word of God and not in the word of man. In this way we will also be able to say to others, 'Come and look at what Scripture says'.

The most helpful Christian writers and the best theologians will always be those who work with the text of Scripture and faithfully expound it. Reading a balance of biblical teaching and systematic exposition we will grow in our understanding of the gospel and develop a biblical spirit as well as a biblical mind.

Historical and biographical reading

We should also read a variety of biographical and historical books. Biographical because Christ reveals his grace in a multicoloured way in his people. When we see others' lives in their wholeness and completeness, we will be stimulated to praise God for that grace and want to imitate the principles that God worked into their lives.

Most Christians who have been serving the Lord for any length of time can pin-point biographies that have made a significant impact on their lives; they have been the right book at the right time for them. Many, like myself, can recall our first reading of *Memoirs and Remains of Robert Murray M'Cheyne*, or Thomas Boston's *Memoirs*, or Arnold Dallimore's wonderful *Life of George Whitefield*. In such biographies we have seen how God transforms and uses his children, and have wanted to follow the example of those who have themselves followed Christ.

We should also read on the larger scale: books about the important events and periods in history of the church; books that cover the whole history of the church in some kind of overview fashion. Why are books on church history so helpful? Because we all have the rather perverse inclination to assume that we are the centre of the world and that our style of Christian thinking and living is identical with the best in every age of the church! But when we read church history we discover that we are making the same mistakes as our forefathers; or perhaps making theological and practical mistakes they avoided!

Another blessing which reading church history brings – or ought to – is to increase within us a spirit of biblical catholicity, and an ability to live with and love those with whom we may disagree on matters that are not essential or central to our Christian living or to our faithfulness to Scripture.

Many of us find contemporary saints more difficult to live with than deceased saints! How true that is when we look down the great roll-call of the heroes of the faith! How many of those whose names trip off our tongues so easily would you *honestly* have found it easy to live with? Think of some who had eccentricities of character, or even failures in doctrine and understanding or in church life.

Why is it that we can tolerate our fellow Christians as long as they are in book form? There is surely an important lesson for us to learn here. Is it because we love them because they loved Christ, and that love covers a multitude of sins? Can we not learn something from this? – to cultivate the balance between a whole-hearted, whole-souled commitment to the truth, and the recognition of the diversity and the weaknesses which exist in God's people. We learn that by reading the history of the church; by reading about the mistakes as well as the triumphs of the past.

Reading church history also helps us to have a long-term perspective. Those who do will be less likely to be impressed by each new fad that sweeps through the church, and more likely to commit themselves to the long-term work of building up the people of God and the kingdom of Christ. Church history teaches us that it is worth building solid foundations if our service is to be lasting.

What else can reading church history do for you? Remember what it did for the Old Testament psalmists so often. It made them turn to God and say, 'Lord! Do it again. Do it again.' The great periods of revival have sometimes begun by people reading about what God had done either in another time or in another place. God has used this to bring to birth a sighing and a longing that he would do it again.

We are all, spiritually, short-sighted. We have believed God's promise, but vaguely. Then we read how God has displayed his sovereign power and grace, and our faith is strengthened. We begin to pray with renewed confidence and zeal that he would show his power again and again. Reading church history can bring us to our knees!

Devotional reading

We should also balance our reading diets with devotional reading; not necessarily 'devotional literature', but books which stir the soul. Wherever you can find reading that stirs your heart, prize it and mark it. Go back to such books again and again; share those books with others. All of us should have certain books in our libraries, no matter how small, to which we can turn when our spirits are low, or our backs are against the wall.

The Christian's spirit can become like a piano that is out of tune. It cannot produce the melody of praise. We feel spiritually desensitised by this world and by our failures in it. We ask God, 'Tune my heart to sing Thy praise'. God sometimes uses books to resensitise us to himself and to his grace, to put our spirits back into tune again.

Why is it that certain books help us in this way? Because they raise our eyes from the cause of our spiritual weakness to the source of spiritual strength and power; they point us to the message of Scripture; the great and glorious Triune God who is strong and active for the blessing of his people.

3: How should we use Christian Literature?

We must use books personally, as we have seen. But we can also use them corporately. Many Christians find great value in reading through a book with their family. Have you ever thought of reading a book with someone else? It is an ideal way to think through its contents, stimulated by and stimulating the Christian friendship.

We can use Christian literature in our church groups, in house groups, study groups or reading groups. It is not only in academic and business seminars that reading may be shared, corporate study and research pursued, or that man- and woman-hours may be put to their best possible use by a pooling of resources.

USING BOOKS PASTORALLY

We should also always be able to use Christian literature pastorally. Our own gifts are limited. Our time is limited. But if we have a working knowledge of our books, we may use them to do, by God's grace, what we ourselves cannot do. That applies not only to those who are ministers and leaders, but to all of us.

If we are to use our books in this way, we must know them. That is one reason why it is better to read selectively but deeply rather than widely but superficially. Know your books! Know specific passages in them. Know those sections which have particularly helped you, so that you are able to point your friends to answers to the questions they ask, and to the help they need. Then you will be able to say to them: 'Here is something that you can read; it will explain to you better, and more clearly than I ever could, what I want to say to you.'

Have books on the existence and nature of God, on the sinfulness of man, on the person and work of Christ, on becoming a Christian, on the Christian life, on death and the life beyond it. You do not need to have a large number of books, so long as you are familiar with those you do have. You may be surprised how rich and fruitful a ministry to others you and your books may have!

In addition to knowing our books, some of us should also be 'showing' our books. Not in the sense of displaying them in bookcases in the living room (not always a good idea!), but by taking the opportunity to introduce younger Christians to the books which have been helpful to ourselves and to others.

Ever since my students days I have been indebted to a minister who took me into his study one day, and told me what he thought of every book in it. Of course not every book he found helpful has proved equally helpful to me. But, thanks to those hours in his study, I had some idea of the books that might be useful in my own Christian life and service. In this sense some Christians have a ministry not only in knowing their books, but in showing them to others.

GIVING CHRISTIAN LITERATURE

Beyond knowing and showing books there is an additional way in which we can make use of Christian literature. We can give sensitively chosen books to friends, in times of need, as gifts on special occasions, or simply as marks of love and appreciation. Books are not cheap; but many good books are still cheaper than records, cassettes and compact discs – and often cheaper than boxes of notepaper!

There are additional ways to give books. In the West, we enjoy a superabundance of Christian literature and a long tradition of having well equipped teachers and preachers. But that is not true in many other parts of the world. Earlier we noted the work of translating Christian literature. Various organizations exist to encourage and finance such translations. Have you, or your church, ever thought of helping such work financially? The needs in many parts of Europe and the East are enormous.

Other organizations can help you to stretch the book purchasing power of your gifts. A number of years ago the Banner of Truth Trust (who publish this and other booklets as well as an extensive list of excellent books) established a Book Fund. Through the Fund, many thousands of books have been given to Christian pastors and leaders throughout the world. Sometimes such men possess only a handful of books before they joyfully open the gift box from the Book Fund. Imagine the joy of seeing your library doubled in a day!

One great incentive to giving in this way is that the publishers are able to enhance the purchasing power of every gift by at least a third and sometimes by as much as one hundred per cent. A gift which would normally purchase two books will be used to purchase three, four or even more books! In the United Kingdom, gifts given by deed of covenant virtually double in purchasing value. Remember Jesus' parable of the talents!*

Do you ever pray about Christian literature? Pray for the work of Christian authors, for writing is usually a lonely business. Pray too for the work of publishers who are genuinely committed to furthering the cause of Christ. Of course profit is essential, otherwise books cannot be published – but pray that publishers will give unrivalled priority to God's glory. Pray for the blessing of God!

What a privilege it is to possess Christian books! We must use them in the best and wisest possible way. There is nowhere that we cannot use it. The ministry of Christian

*Details of the Book Fund will be found at the end of this booklet.

books is one in which all of us – rich and poor, old and young, highly educated or poorly educated – can share. Make sure you are always reading and using good books!

If he shall not lose his reward, who gives a cup of cold water to his thirsty neighbour, what will not be the reward of those who by putting good books into the hands of those neighbours open to them the fountains of eternal life?

Thomas à Kempis

The following selection of *paperbacks* and *booklets* from the publisher will provide a basic library for reading and giving.

BIBLE STUDY

J. Gresham Machen, *The New Testament*. A clear, readable introduction to the books of the New Testament. Highly recommended.

Geoffrey Thomas, *Reading the Bible*. Wise counsel on how to read and study the Bible for yourself. Includes a Bible reading programme.

Geoffrey Wilson, *The New Testament Commentary Series* (paperback commentaries on Paul's letters).

CHRISTIAN DOCTRINE

L. Berkhof, *Summary of Christian Doctrine*. A guidebook to the teaching of the Bible on all of the major Christian doctrines.

C. Brown, *The Divine Glory of Christ*. A fine, brief study of the person of Jesus Christ.

W.J. Grier, *The Momentous Event*. An exposition of biblical teaching on the events of the future.

R.B. Kuiper, *The Glorious Body of Christ*. A very readable book containing many fine chapters on the nature of the church.

D.M. Lloyd-Jones, *Authority*. A study of the authority of Scripture and the work of the Holy Spirit which has helped many Christians.

John Murray, *Redemption – Accomplished and Applied*. A rich and careful exposition of the work of Christ and its application. Requires and repays thoughtful reading.

J.G. Machen, *The Christian View of Man*. A popularly written study by one of the most significant Christian leaders and scholars in the 20th century.

Hugh Martin, *The Shadow of Calvary*. A famous study of the suffering and death of Christ.

George Smeaton, *The Doctrine of the Holy Spirit*. A rich study of the ministry of the Holy Spirit.

Thomas Watson, *A Body of Divinity*. A classic exposition of Christian doctrine.

E.J. Young, *Genesis 3*. A popular study by a great Old Testament scholar on one of the most vital chapters in the Bible.

E. J. Young, *Thy Word is Truth*. A careful, scholarly but popular study of the inspiration, authority and reliability of the Bible.

CHRISTIAN LIVING

Walter J. Chantry, *The Shadow of the Cross*. A challenging study of the Christian life.

Sinclair B. Ferguson, *The Christian Life*. Expounds and applies the biblical doctrines surrounding the Christian life.

Sinclair B. Ferguson, *Discovering God's Will*. Discusses general principles of guidance and applies them to such areas as vocation and marriage.

D.B. Knox, *Not By Bread Alone*. Discussions of important contemporary moral and social issues by a well-known Australian theologian.

D.M. Lloyd-Jones, *Life in the Spirit*. A vigorous exposition of Paul's practical teaching in Ephesians 5:18–6:9.

John J. Murray, *Behind a Frowning Providence*. A very helpful modern booklet on suffering and trials.

John Newton, *The Letters of John Newton*. A wonderful selection of letters giving spiritual counsel, written by the famous hymn-writer who was once a slave-trader.

Daniel Wray, *The Importance of the Local Church*. A booklet on the importance of church membership.

BIOGRAPHIES

J. Purves, *Fair Sunshine*, A much-loved and widely-read

series of pen-portraits of the martyred Scottish Covenanters.

J.C. Ryle, *Christian Leaders of the Eighteenth Century*. Short and well-written accounts of some great Christian leaders in a dramatic period of church history.

John Sargent, *The Life of Henry Martyn*. One of the most famous missionary biographies ever written.

THE BANNER OF TRUTH TRUST
BOOK FUND

A practical way to share in the ministry of Christian literature throughout the world.

The Fund distributes books to pastors and Christian leaders throughout the world.

Contributions to the Book Fund effectively increase the purchasing power of your gift by 33%. e.g. a gift of £15 will purchase £20 of books from the Trust's catalogue.

Contributions given by Deed of Covenant will almost double the purchasing power of your gift.

Gifts, or requests for further information should be directed to:

THE BOOK FUND
THE BANNER OF TRUTH TRUST
3 MURRAYFIELD ROAD
EDINBURGH EH12 6EL

SOME OTHER
BANNER OF TRUTH
TITLES

THE CHRISTIAN LIFE
A Doctrinal Introduction

Sinclair B. Ferguson

'Christian doctrine matters for Christian living.' This is 'one of the most important growth points of the Christian life', writes Sinclair B. Ferguson. From this starting point, *The Christian Life* expounds such key biblical themes as grace, faith, repentance, new birth and assurance with clarity and contagious enthusiasm. 'Christian doctrines are life-shaping', explains the author, because 'they show us the God we worship'.

Widely used and appreciated since its first appearance, *The Christian Life* not only expounds the teaching of Scripture, but outlines its meaning for practical Christian living.

ISBN 0 85151 516 9
240pp. Paperback.

THE SERMON ON THE MOUNT
Kingdom Life in a Fallen World

Sinclair B. Ferguson

The Sermon on the Mount is probably the best known section of the entire Bible. Yet it is also one of the least understood parts of the teaching of Jesus Christ. 'It is not a sermon about an ideal life in an ideal world' writes Sinclair B. Ferguson, 'but about the kingdom life in a fallen world'. It answers some of the most pressing questions that every Christian encounters: What is a Christian? Does the Law of God still have a place in the Christian life? How can I learn to pray? How can I learn self-discipline? Why am I a prisoner to anxiety?

The Sermon on the Mount deals with these issues in a crisp, concise and readable way. It provides an ideal introduction to Jesus' great manifesto for life in his kingdom.

ISBN 0 85151 519 3
184pp. Paperback.

GROW IN GRACE

Sinclair B. Ferguson

Becoming a Christian is only the beginning of a process of spiritual growth that involves a continual increase in a knowledge of God, an obedience to his word and an understanding of his will. Yet, some Christian's lives seem to grind slowly to a halt, while others are disappointed because their spiritual progress has not been as straightforward or as rapid as they had hoped. The growth of others is stunted by a lack of proper spiritual nourishment. Yet others feel they do not understand how to become mature Christians.

Grow in Grace explains how God helps us to develop as members of his family. Taking Jesus himself as the model for our growth, it explains some of the biblical principles of spiritual development, and gives a number of 'case histories' to illustrate how God works in our lives to mature us as Christians.

ISBN 0 85151 557 6
160pp. Paperback.

A HEART FOR GOD

Sinclair B. Ferguson

A Heart For God is written out of the conviction that the world's greatest need, and the contemporary church's greatest lack is the knowledge of God. In a popular, readable style it draws us to an awareness of the character of God and the nature of his relationship to his people.

In these pages, Sinclair B. Ferguson guides us, step-by-step, to see the greatness of God in his majesty and creating power; to sense the tenderness of his care and the marvel of his love. *A Heart For God* is 'Practical, pastoral and profound' (J. I. Packer). It unfolds the grace of God with a simple clarity which should lead each reader to pray (with John Calvin, the reformer): 'I offer my heart to you, Lord, eagerly and earnestly.'

ISBN 0 85151 502 9
144pp. Paperback.

CHILDREN OF THE LIVING GOD

Sinclair B. Ferguson

Jesus Christ taught his disciples to call God 'Our Father', and to live as members of his family. Although simple enough for every Christian to understand this is also so profound that its implications take a lifetime to explore fully.

Children of the Living God takes as its starting point the wise and thought-provoking question of an old writer: 'If the love of a father will not make a child delight in him, what will?' It underlines that we were created for joyful fellowship with God, and explains how we enter his family by new birth and adoption. Its chapters show how the Spirit of sonship, Christian freedom, divine discipline, prayer and the sacraments all contribute to our experience of the love the Father has for his children.

ISBN 0 85151 526 3
144pp. Paperback.

DISCOVERING GOD'S WILL

Sinclair B. Ferguson

There are few more important things in the Christian's life than *Discovering God's Will*. The assurance that we are in the centre of God's purposes brings lasting stability to our experience.

But how do we discover the will of God for our lives?

Sinclair Ferguson answers this question by showing how God's will is shaped by his ultimate purposes for us. *Discovering God's Will* draws out fundamental principles by which God guides us, applies them to practical situations like vocation and marriage, and underlines many important biblical counsels. It shows that the guidance God gives comes primarily through knowing, loving and obeying him.

ISBN 0 85151 344 4
128pp. Paperback.

Other booklets in this series:

The Authentic Gospel, *Jeffrey E. Wilson*

Behind a Frowning Providence, *John J. Murray*

Biblical Church Discipline, *Daniel Wray*

The Carnal Christian, *E. C. Reisinger*

Christians Grieve Too, *D. Howard*

Coming to Faith in Christ, *John Benton*

The Cross – The Vindication of God, *D. M. Lloyd-Jones*

The Five Points of Calvinism, *W. J. Seaton*

Healthy Christian Growth, *Sinclair B. Ferguson*

The Importance of The Local Church, *D. Wray*

The Incomparable Book, *W. McDowell*

The Invitation System, *Iain H. Murray*

Is There an Answer? *Roger Ellsworth*

A Life of Principled Obedience, *A. N. Martin*

Living the Christian Life, *A. N. Martin*

The Moral Basis of Faith, *Tom Wells*

Open Your Mouth for the Dumb, *Peter Barnes*

Origins? *R. B. Ranganathan*

The Practical Implications of Calvinism, *A. N. Martin*

Reading the Bible, *Geoffrey Thomas*

Seeing Jesus, *Peter Barnes*

Victory: The Work of the Spirit, *P. Potgieter*

What's Wrong With Preaching Today?, *A. N. Martin*

For free illustrated catalogue please write to
THE BANNER OF TRUTH TRUST
3 Murrayfield Road, Edinburgh EH12 6EL
PO Box 621, Carlisle, Pennsylvania 17013, U.S.A.